Taking Your Camera to

MEXICO

Ted Park

Steadwell Books

Raintree Steck-Vaughn Publishers

A Harcourt Company

Austin · New York

www.steck-vaughn.com

Published by Raintree Steck-Vaughn Publishers,
an imprint of Steck-Vaughn Company

Library of Congress Cataloging-in-Publication Data
Park, Ted
    Mexico/ by Ted Park.
        p. cm. — (Taking your camera to)
    Summary: Introduces the geography, points of interest, way of life, economy, culture, and people of Mexico.
    ISBN 0-7398-1804-X
    1. Mexico—Juvenile literature. 2. Mexico—Pictorial works—Juvenile literature.
[1. Mexico.] I. Title. II. Series.

F1208.5.P33 2000   *96620*
972—dc21   99-058643

Printed in the United States of America
10 9 8 7 6 5 4 3 2 1 W 03 02 01 00

Photo acknowledgments

Cover ©Bruce Stoddard/FPG International; p.1 ©Peter Gridley/FPG International; p.3a ©Danny Lehman/CORBIS; p.3b ©Travelpix/FPG International; p.3c ©Suzanne Murphy-Larronde/FPG International; p.3d ©Peter Gridley/FPG International; p.5 ©Danny Lehman/CORBIS; p.8 ©Harvey Lloyd/FPG International; p.9 ©Travelpix/FPG International; p.11 ©Vladimir Pcholkin/FPG International; p.13 ©Peter Gridley/FPG International; p.15a ©Suzanne Murphy-Larronde/FPG International; pp.15b, 17a ©iSwoop/FPG International; p.17b ©PhotoDisc; p.19 ©Danny Lehman/CORBIS; p.21a ©Travelpix/FPG International; p.21b ©Phil Schermeister/CORBIS; p.23 ©AFP/CORBIS; p.25 ©iSwoop/FPG International; p.27 ©Chris Salvo/FPG International; p.28a ©Vladimir Pcholkin/FPG International; p.28b ©Danny Lehman/CORBIS; p.29a ©PhotoDisc; p.29b ©Travelpix/FPG International; p.29c ©Harvey Lloyd/FPG International.

All statistics in the Quick Facts section come from *The New York Times Almanac* (1999) and *The World Almanac* (1999).

Contents

This Is Mexico

Mexico is a very old country. People lived in Mexico more than 2,000 years ago. They built big cities. They made beautiful works of art. If you took your camera to Mexico, you could photograph some of these ancient things.

Mexico also has many modern cities. One of them is Guadalajara. It is the second largest city in Mexico. Guadalajara has a cathedral. A cathedral is a large church. The city also has many stores. Some of the shops are outside. People sell food, clothes, souvenirs, and other things at these outdoor markets. If you walked along the streets of Guadalajara, you could find many interesting sights to photograph.

In this book you will see some things that are very old. Other things that you see are new. This book will tell you a lot about the country of Mexico.

An open-air market in Guadalajara

 4

# The Place

Mexico is a large country. It is about 2,000 miles (3,218 km) from north to south. This is about three times the size of Texas. Mexico is much wider at the north than it is at the south. The United States is to the north of Mexico. To the south are the Central American countries of Guatemala and Belize. The Pacific Ocean is to the west. The Gulf of Mexico and the Caribbean Sea are to the east.

A strip of land called Baja California runs down the west side of the country. *Baja* is Spanish for "lower." Baja California is a peninsula. This is a piece of land that has water on three sides. On the east side of Mexico is another peninsula. This is called the Yucatán Peninsula.

Las Vegas

Los Alamos, Santa Fe

Albuquerque

Los Angeles

Phoenix

Roswell

UNITED STATES Dallas

San Diego Mexicali

Las Cruces

Tucson

El Paso

Temple

Austin

Baton Rouge

Birmingham

Pensacola

Hermosillo

Chihuahua

Del Rio

San Antonio

Houston
Galveston

New Orleans

MEXICO

Saltillo Monterrey

Gulf of Mexico

Culiacan

La Paz

Durango

Ciudad Victoria

Zacatecas

Aguascalientes San Luis Potosi

Tepic Leon

Merida

Guadalajara

Queretaro

Pachuca

Campeche

Morelia

Colima ★ **Mexico City**

Toluca Puebla

Chetumal

Villahermosa

Belize City

Chilpancingo

Oaxaca

Belmopan
★ **BELIZE**

Tuxtla Gutierrez

GUATEMALA

Mexico

⊕ National Capital

Leon • City

Internaional Boundary

200 km

0   200 Miles

N

P a c i f i c   O c e a n

Guatemala ★

HONDURAS
Tegucig ★

7

Mexico has two mountain chains. They are on each side of the country. These mountains are the western and eastern Sierra Madre mountains. There is a plateau between these mountains. A plateau is a flat area of land that is higher than the land around it. Mexico also has flat plains along the coast. In the south there are volcanoes.

Mexico has many mountains.

The city of Acapulco is on the Pacific Ocean.

Temperatures in the northern part of Mexico are cool. Because there is little rain, the land there is dry. In the south the weather is hot and rainy. Plants and trees grow very fast in this kind of weather. Much of southern Mexico is covered with thick forests known as rain forests.

Mexico has many earthquakes. A bad earthquake hit Mexico City in 1985. There have been several smaller ones since then.

Mexico City

Mexico City is the capital of Mexico. It is the country's largest city. There are many tall new buildings in Mexico City. There are also smaller ones that were built hundreds of years ago.

One of the most popular places in Mexico City is the Plaza de la Constitución. It is a large open area. It is also called the Zócalo. On one side of the plaza is a very big church. This church was built more than 400 years ago.

Behind the church are the ruins, or pieces, of a very old temple. A temple is like a church. This was the main temple of a powerful group of native people called Aztecs. The Aztecs lived in Mexico around A.D. 1200. They ruled Mexico for hundreds of years.

These are just some of the places in Mexico City that you can photograph with your camera.

Mexico City is one of the world's largest cities.

Places to Visit

There are many ruins that you can photograph. One famous one is the Pyramid of the Sun, in the city of Teotihuacán. A pyramid is a building with four sides that come to a point at the top. The building is 230 feet (70 m) high.

Many groups of native peoples lived in Mexico. The most famous were the Maya. They lived in Mexico from 300 B.C. to A.D. 900. Many of their buildings are still standing. Some of them are in Chichén Itzá. This is a place on the Yucatán Peninsula. If you took your camera there, you could photograph Mayan temples and statues.

In 1519 a Spanish explorer came to Mexico. His name was Hernán Cortés. He brought many soldiers with him. Cortés met Montezuma, who was the leader of the Aztecs. They met in the city of Tenochtitlán, the Aztec capital. Mexico City is built on top of Tenochtitlán.

Cortés and his soldiers fought with the Aztecs. The Spanish won. By 1521 the Spanish controlled all of Mexico. They ruled the country for the next 300 years.

 12

The Mexicans wanted to be free from Spain, and by 1821 they were. An important place in Mexico City is the Monument of National Independence. A monument is built to remind people of something important. This monument reminds people that the Mexican people had to fight to be free.

Mexico has many Mayan pyramids that can still be seen today.

 # The People

There are almost 99 million people living in Mexico. About 60 percent of them are mestizos. Mestizos are not Spanish. They are not Native Americans either. They are a mixture of both of these peoples. They think of themselves as Mexicans.

The rest of the Mexican people are either native peoples or Hispanic. A Hispanic is a person whose ancestors are from Spain, Portugal, or Latin America. Almost all Mexicans speak Spanish. In fact, more Spanish-speaking people live in Mexico than anywhere else in the world.

Many Mexicans move to the United States. They go there to look for work and a new life. Many Mexicans go to California, Texas, and Florida. Immigrants also come to Mexico from Central America.

Today most Mexicans are mestizos.

A young man in traditional costume

15

Life in Mexico

Most Mexicans live in cities. They come to the cities to look for jobs. About 20 million people live in and around Mexico City. This is almost one-fifth of all the people living in the entire country.

Many Mexicans have large families. This means there are many young people in Mexico. Families live together in small houses or apartments. Grandparents often take care of the children so that both parents can work. Some families have cars.

Almost one-fourth of all Mexicans are farmers. Most of the work on the farms is done by hand.

In the countryside, many Mexican farmers use donkeys to carry their goods to market.

Many Mexicans live in cities.

Government and Religion

Mexico's official name is the United Mexican States. Mexico is a republic. This means that the people of Mexico elect the president, or leader. The president is elected for six years. The Mexicans also elect the people who help the president run the country. The group of people that makes the laws is called Congress. It is made up of the Senate and the Chamber of Deputies. The president is the leader of Congress.

Most Mexicans are Roman Catholic. They follow the teachings of the Catholic church. However, they also keep some ancient religious customs of the native peoples. A custom is something that has been done for a long time. One native custom is to decorate religious statues with flowers. In Mexico these customs have mixed with the teachings of the Catholic church.

There are many beautiful cathedrals in Mexico that you can photograph. This is the cathedral in Mexico City.

Earning a Living

Many of Mexico's farms are in the south. Corn is the most important crop. Farmers grow tropical fruits, sugarcane, and wheat. Other important products are chicle and cacao. Chicle is used to make chewing gum. Cacao is used to make chocolate.

In the north, cattle are raised. Fishing is also an important industry, especially along Mexico's coasts.

Mexico has many natural resources. These are things that come from nature and are useful to people. These include gold, silver, and copper. Oil is another natural resource. It is found along Mexico's east coast. Today Mexico is the sixth largest producer of the world's oil. Mining, or digging, for these resources makes jobs.

The tourist industry also provides many jobs. People from all over the world come to visit Mexico. They like the sunny beaches. They enjoy seeing the ancient Mayan and Aztec places. They like to buy the jewelry and pottery that Mexicans are famous for making.

Tourists watch cliff divers in **Acapulco.**

A farmer plows a field in **Mexico.**

School and Sports

Young people in Mexico are supposed to go to school from ages 6 to 14. But half of them quit school by the time they are 11. Many children don't go to school at all. They must help their families at home. About one-fourth of the students stay in school until they are 17. Then they may go to college. Other students may go to schools that teach skills to workers.

Mexico City University is the oldest and largest university in the country. It was founded in 1551. About 300,000 students go to classes there. The school is so large that many students have to use taxis to get from one class to another.

Mexico's favorite sport is soccer. It is often called by its Spanish name, *fútbol*. Young people play soccer in groups after school. The Mexican people like to watch soccer games. As many as 100,000 people go to Aztec

Stadium in Mexico City to watch games played by their favorite teams.

Volleyball is another popular sport. Rodeos and bullfighting are also popular among many Mexicans. The Spanish brought these two sports to Mexico many years ago.

Soccer is very popular in Mexico.

23

Food and Holidays

Mexican food is simple and tasty. Tortillas are thin pancakes that are made of corn flour. They are steamed. Then they are filled with cheese, beans, and a spicy sauce. Another favorite food is tacos. These are fried tortillas filled with cheese and beans.

One of the biggest holidays in Mexico is the Day of the Dead. It is on November 2. This is a religious holiday that is also called the Feast of All Souls. People honor the dead with dancing, toys, and food. They even make candies that look like skulls and skeletons.

At Christmas, children get piñatas. These are hollow shapes made of many layers of paper glued together. They are painted on the outside. Piñatas are filled with little toys and candies. The children try to break them open with a stick. When they do, they get their prizes.

Mexicans have fiestas throughout the year. A fiesta is a big party with dancing, music, and food.

Making tortillas

The Future

If you took your camera to Mexico, you would see a country where there are modern, or new, things right next to things that are very old.

Mexico exports, or sends, many kinds of natural resources to other countries. This brings money into the country. It also makes jobs for Mexican people.

The people of Mexico are hardworking. They want to make Mexico an even better place to live in and to visit than it is now. When you leave the country, a Mexican is likely to say to you "*Hasta la vista.*" In English, this means "See you again."

Oil rigs that are off the shore in the Gulf of Mexico

Quick Facts About
MEXICO

Capital
Mexico City

Borders
United States to the north (the states that border Mexico are Texas, New Mexico, Arizona, and California). Belize and Guatemala to the south

Area
761,603 square miles
(1,972,400 sq km)

Population
98,552,776

Largest cities
Mexico City (8,236,960 people);
Guadalajara (1,628,617 people);
Monterrey (1,064,917 people)

Chief crops
corn, wheat, soybeans, rice, beans

Natural resources
crude oil, silver, copper, gold, lead

Longest river
Rio Bravo, known as Rio Grande in the United States. 2,439 miles (3,925 km)

28

Flag of Mexico

Coastline
5,798 miles (9,329 km)

Monetary unit
peso

Literacy rate
90 percent of Mexicans can
read and write

Major industries
food and beverages, tobacco,
chemicals

Glossary

Aztecs (AZ-teks) A powerful group of native people who lived in Mexico around A.D. 1200

Baja California (BA-ha) A peninsula on the western side of Mexico

Chichén Itzá (CHICH-chen it-SAH) A place on the Yucatán Peninsula that has Mayan temples and statues

Congress The group that makes the laws in Mexico

fútbol (FUT-bohl) The Spanish word for soccer

Guadalajara (gwad-uh-luh-HAR-uh) The second largest city in Mexico

Hispanic (his-PAN-ik) A person whose ancestors came from Spain, Portugal, or Latin America

Maya (MY-uh) A well-known group of native people who lived in Mexico from 300 B.C. to A.D. 900

mestizos (meh-STEE-zos) Mexicans who have both Spanish and Native American ancestors

Mexico City The capital of Mexico, and its largest city

Monument of National Independence An important place in Mexico City built to remind people that Mexicans fought for their freedom

 30

peninsula (puh-NIN-suh-luh) An area of land that has water on three sides

piñatas (peen-YAHT-uhs) Hollow shapes that are made of hard paper and filled with little toys

plateau (plah-TOW) A flat area of land that is higher than the land around it

Plaza de la Constitución (con-sti-too-SEEOWN) One of the most popular places in Mexico City

pyramid (PIR-uh-mid) A building with four sides that come to a point at the top

Pyramid of the Sun A famous ruin in Teotihuacán

rain forest A place where trees are very tall and close together and many different plants and animals live

tacos (TAK-oz) Fried tortillas filled with cheese and beans

Tenochtitlán (tay-noch-tee-TLON) The capital of the Aztec Empire, which is now the site of Mexico City

Teotihuacán (tay-oh-tee-wuh-KON) A city in central Mexico

tortillas (tor-TEE-uhz) Pancakes made of corn flour

Yucatán Peninsula (yuh-kuh-TON) A peninsula on the eastern side of Mexico

Zócalo (ZOW-kuh-low) The Plaza de la Constitución

31

Index